Prison Segmentation for Prison Tourism

New Eyes On Everything

Rev. Mike Wanner

Copyright
Rev. Mike Wanner

October 4, 2018

Selected Images Used by License

"Prison Presents" Tab
"Healing Presents" Tab

http://www.AngelRaphaelSpeaks.com

Table Of Contents

Copyright 2
Table Of Contents 3
Introduction 4
1 - Why I am Writing This Book 5
2 - What is Prison Tourism? 6
3 - We Need To Reassess Our Priorities 7
4 - Survival Challenges 8
5 - Communities Overlap 9
6 - A Holistic Paradyme Shift is Indicated 10
7 - Stop The Bleeding First 11
8 - Social Disconnection Stifles Possibilities 12
9 - Tourists Are Attracted To Prison Stories 13
10 - America Could Upgrade Everything 16
11 - What Can We Gain by Prison Tourism? 19
12 – Business Ramp-Up Possibilities 20
13 - Possible Prisoner Skill Highlighting 21
14 - Prison Tourist Family Time Plusses 22
15 - Prison Tourism Wrap-Up 23
16 - Thank You 24
17 - Don't Worry Ever 25
18 - Books Category Resources 26
19 - Angels Please Prayers 27
20 - Private Channeling 28
21 - Reverend Mike Wanner 29

Introduction

I have been writing a lot about prisons and realized that much of the complexity is rooted in a constant of slowness for any change even to be possible. While in business, reassessment is continuously necessary to attain an optimistic perspective that can motivate people to do their best, the prison community seems to be more focused on the literal interpretation of the rulings that were issued in the past as they are required to do by law.

The rigidity of the rules makes every change complicated, and that can mean costly and slow. The goals that are referenced repeatedly throughout stories in the press are about the need for fair treatment, rehabilitation and avoiding recidivism.

It seems that recidivism is staying high and rehabilitation seems to be staying minimal, and that is not cost effective for the prisons, judicial system or the taxpayers.

My observations keep returning me to the need for shifting the process of inviting change. The reality is that the methods of prison change are not typical or user-friendly.

Blame is not something that can be productive in prison change. Cooperation and creativity are areas that I could stimulate change. I believe that streamlining processes for reform can change many things if we can put prisoners in activities where they earn the right to take steps on their paths toward freedom.

1 - Why I am Writing This Book

I have been absolutely amazed at the complexity of the whole prison situation and the variety of rules and authorities that are required to oversee the various facilities.

I offer some ideas here for consideration. My thoughts will probably not seem practical, and they may not be in many facilities because of design differences, regulating authorities and geographical variables.

I intend to fully root this book and all my others in the respect that each individual desires and deserves. Respect for many people in our society is not given because the one who could offer it may lack the understanding of what it is and how one shows it to other people.

All too often recently, you hear people demand respect, and within that demand, they lack respect for the one who they wish to show it to them. When I read about the prisons and the courts and the treatment of prisoners, I am always aware of the impersonal nature of the dialogue.

In my experience, a little consideration goes a long way. I invite readers to self-test themselves for sensitivity to others.

A good reason to be respectful is that it is the right thing to do. Another excellent reason to do it is that it can be much less stressful and much more productive for all.

Respectful treatment may not be optimal in prisons. More transparency stimulated by tourism could help that.

2 - What is Prison Tourism?

Travelers or tourists are those who are traveling to and stay in places outside their usual home on a temporary basis for one or many reasons that may include emergency circumstances like a refuge or medical care or business or leisure or adventure or any particular interest.

Adding Prison before tourism brings the destination into particular relevance. Seeking the peace of mind for a family member or prisoner may be a noble reason to be a prison tourist, but it can also realign societal understanding about everything that could help the prisoners and the staff.

Other reasons to do that could be a societal revitalization of values that could help the need for more prisons to be stifled. Working to increase the productivity of prisons toward rehabilitating those who are there can also be mutually beneficial.

The emphasis here is many faceted and could have a significant impact in areas of states with populations where there are substantial numbers of prisoners who have a family who could visit them if there were economical options available to facilitate the process.

Prison tourism could also be an economic opportunity for businesses to develop efforts which could help the prison community, the rehabilitation of prisoners and provide needed relief for taxpayers by maintaining stimulation of networks that could help them provide opportunities for prisoners when they exit.

3 - We Need To Reassess Our Priorities

The statistics of incarceration in America exceed the numbers of all other countries, and that is not something in which we can take pride.

I was born in the impressive City of Philadelphia in the great State of Pennsylvania, and there were many inventions and institutions that were birthed here. One institution was the world's First Penitentiary which was also the largest and the most expensive building in the United States at the time.

Eastern State Penitentiary opened in 1829, and it featured a system of solitary confinement where prisoners were locked in single cells and prevented from all form of social interaction.

The prison closed in 1971, and it should be evident that the developers were gone long before the doors closed. The history continues to be referenced, and the impact of solitary confinement is still discussed as to all the pros and cons of its use.

Solitary is a good indication of the complexity of prison restructuring. Almost two hundred years later and the horsepower of change is minimal.

Shall we work on accelerating the changes that can save the taxpayers money and reconnect families? Human connectivity through social networks can do the job when an acceleration plan is in place.

4 - Survival Challenges

Survival in prisons can offer many challenges that non-participants and non-residents do not understand. While there are rules established by the administration, there are also expectations that are not written but may be equally enforceable by participants in certain cultures.

It seems that resistance to everything and everybody persists in a way that is anathema to stress-free living so that incarceration places are a potential explosive human environment. When stress is so high, the discovery of an optimal remedial plan may be less than obvious.

Throughout the broader law enforcement system, there seems to be a lack of understanding for the sensitivity of the humans that interact with enforcement officials. Some institution staffs are spotlighted as being corrupt and inadequately trained while the problems associated with each example may not be institutional, but social.

At so many levels, our society displays avoidance strategies and ostracisation as the preferred method of disposal of human interactions that are less than optimal. These absolute values do not solve problems if they are not comprehensive enough to embrace the consequences of the remediations performed.

Solving one problem by creating another is not beneficial to the broader society. It seems apparent that we need to take a long-range view of the causes and effects within our communities.

5 - Communities Overlap

In our cities, there are many neighborhoods, and each can have definable patterns that tolerate different things more than their neighbors. Media can stimulate different things in different areas and have varied results.

Heavy-handedness by authorities can rile the constituents and disrupt communities at the core level. Our politicians in recent years do not seem as adept at negotiations as their predecessors.

In politics, there was always a need for statesmanship and transparency so that logic could prevail over time. The isolation of citizens from the political and financial consequences is a significant cause of our current day troubles.

Prisons and our societies are so very complicated that it is very challenging to be able to understand the simplified version of what needs to be done. Nobody yet can project the answers to the societal problems that have created the environment that we live in where so much is messed up and unmanageable.

The Angel's request of me was to visit prison energetically and bring back information to the angels who have now influenced a finessing of my assignment to offer concepts for consideration. I am trying as best I can while still trying to stay balanced myself, but one person is not enough to make a satisfactory effort, so I am asking for the readers to join the effort and bring your ideas forward.

Every layer of the Judicial system should be considered for enhancement.

6 - A Holistic Paradyme Shift is Indicated

The marginalization of many multitudes through Mass Incarceration is Unsustainable, so we need to get to work to change our world as we know it. We need new priorities.

Needing new priorities does not mean that it will be easy as everything related to prisons is somewhat entrenched at many levels so deliberate efforts formatted in a consistently positive way can push the agenda forward a bit. Persistent positive efforts can build leadership so that you can continue to be a positive force for the whole community.

Engaging with community organizations can really involve the community in the discussion about changing the facilities and bring expert outsiders to the panel of contributors to the process.

We Need To Reassess Our Priorities

1. Constitutional
2. Parenting
3. Education
4. Incarceration
5. Law Enforcement

7 - Stop The Bleeding First

We
Are
Hemorrhaging
The
Quality
Of
American
Life
Now

8 - Social Disconnection Stifles Possibilities

There is no way to know the communication realities for any given facility, but the constant reports of contraband cell phones would lead one to think that there is a demand for reconnecting with the broader world. Encouraging creativity could change a lot in prison in a way that many people can benefit.

Here is my take on why little changes seem stuck:

Blaming Authorities Is A Pattern That Helps Nobody And Changes Nothing

Teamwork is Minimal

People who deserve blame are already dead.

Prison tourism could have a dynamic shift if enough facilities were focused on positive possibilities. We could encourage significant interactive efforts.

The statistics of incarceration in America exceed the numbers of all other countries, and that is not something in which we can take pride.

9 - Tourists Are Attracted To Prison Stories

Three Examples of Popular Sites

Alcatraz Island

Juan Manuel de Ayala, a Spanish explorer named Alcatraz Isla de Los Alcatraces (Isle of the Pelicans), which sounds like a resort.

The site was sold to the United States Government in 1849 and five years later was the site of the First Lighthouse on the California coast. A US Army detachment was housed there in 1859, and in 1861 it was designated for military offenders.

It later became a federal prison that operated from 1934 - 1963.

The facility housed many of the American Prison dignitaries including mob czar Al Capone, bank robber George "Machine Gun" Kelly and Robert Stroud, "The Birdman" of Hollywood movie fame.

Visitors can now listen to an audio tour while inspecting the cells or in the deserted exercise yard and learn about the Indian occupation from 1969-71, carried out in part to press their land claims.

It has been many years since I visited but I remember well the Red and White Ferry fleet that facilitated the transport element to get visitors from the mainland to the Island and back.

There was such symbolism of landing on the Island and filing off the boat one by one and moving up the trail to the prison.

Alcatraz Island

Old Melbourne Gaol, Australia

Built in the mid-1800s when the Victorian gold rushes created a crime surge, Old Melbourne Gaol (Old English Spelling) held petty offenders, homeless people and the mentally ill as well as dangerous criminals.

It saw 133 executions. The most famous was the bushranger Ned Kelly, hanged in 1880 for the murders of three police officers. One of his death masks is on display there.

Though closed as a prison in 1929, it wasn't until 1972 that the site was taken over by the National Trust.
Visitors can now take self-guided tours to see what prison life was like or go on organized ghost tours for a different perspective.

Eastern State Penitentiary, United States

From its opening in 1829, Eastern State Penitentiary in Philadelphia was controversial for its system of total solitary confinement.

After his visit in 1842, Charles Dickens wrote: "The System is rigid, strict and hopeless ... and I believe it to be cruel and wrong."

The prison closed in 1970, has become a tourist attraction. Unlike the early tours, when visitors wore hard hats, there's now an audio tour narrated by actor Steve Buscemi that lets the curious explore behind the grim, castle-like walls, listening to former guards and inmates describe life at Eastern State.

Eastern State is famous for their **Terror Behind the Walls** – A totally haunting attraction.

www.easternstate.org

10 - America Could Upgrade Everything

Earlier in this book, I mentioned that we need to reassess our priorities. I wrote It seems that we have some things to change:

1. Constitutional
2. Parenting
3. Education
4. Incarceration
5. Law Enforcement

A - Constitutional

We could use a rewrite of our enabling laws around the law enforcement and judicial processes. The old rules seem to be utterly unwieldy within the reality of current times.

Communications have improved, and tempers have truncated with lessened patience, so the general public is a lot less tolerant of bureaucratic processes. While there is no legitimate entitlement to expedient procedures in government, common sense could enhance the concept that diligence is expected and service is also.

We could use a rewrite of our enabling laws around the process of law enforcement. It seems that the entire world of America relies on Television for emotional balance guidance and that does not seem to translate well in the real world, so dysfunctional perspective appears to rule.

While it seems that those arrested have an appearance of representation, common sense will make it clear for those who wish to consider it, that Challenges are many. Comprehension by scared first-timers in the legal process could help communications and service to the broader community.

While we need laws which helpt to provide order to our society, we also need sufficient understanding and sensitivity to those who are not fully mature and informed of the consequence of folly.

B - Parenting

Parenting is a crucial component to all levels of our society. Unfortunately, there seems to be a lack of proficiency in the ability to parent, and that can cause the children great struggles.

About 2.7 million children of prisoners can have an especially hard time as the separation from Mom or Dad can cause severe episodes of inadequate support.

C - Education

The struggling children of prisoners can interact with other children and complicate the educational resource challenges. There is a whole book about prisoners advising the innercity teachers in this series.

Little bits of information can make a huge difference for children and their teachers and the communities that house the schools.

D - Incarceration

An evaluation is needed to determine whether incarceration works enough to justify the expense. We need to know:
1. What is Working?
2. What is not working?
3. What can we change to enhance results?
4. What can we adjust to bring frugal and productive changes?
5. How we can support safety for staff.
6. What can we do to increase safety for residents?

E - Law Enforcement

An evaluation is needed to determine whether Law Enforcement works well enough to help mitigate the need for incarceration. We need to know:

1. What is Working?
2. What is not working?
3. What can we change to enhance results?
4. What can we adjust to being frugal and productive messaging to the citizens?
5. How can we support safety for Officer and citizens?
6. What can we do to be frugal and effective?

11 - What Can We Gain by Prison Tourism?

More open communication between communities and prisons could be a giant step forward for both. Interaction is limited now, and the demand for connecting is quite clear.

Appropriateness of communication and the effects of those messages can be problematic for the facilities. The total withholding of discussions is also questionable for the facilities.

Balanced opportunities for monitored solid messaging can be pivotal to revitalizing the prospects for rehabilitation. When someone is staving, a little food can help them keep going.

When someone feels isolated alone and vulnerable, a little bit of hope can help them keep going. When we develop a plan to open a window and allow some fresh air, stagnancy can flow away.

We should be able to develop some progress opportunities for new and supervised normalization tools that can sooth the isolation, enhance hope and bring about more compatible interactions.

There can be many ways that we can use tourist approaches to revitalize lives and hope that all could reduce resistance and violence. I believe there is a lot that can be done and I write about it all and offer it free as often as I can.

I invite every reader to write a dialogue about real hope for prisoners. Read about how to at
http://angelraphaelspeaks.com/prison-possible/

12 – Business Ramp-Up Possibilities

Prison Tourism could provide an opportunity for Businesses to present opportunities to the residents.

A Well-formatted event could invite businesses to present their companies as a series of opportunities for prisoners to consider upon re-entry.

Creating a friendly format for interaction between deserving prisoners and the world could be a giant step forward for the normalization of them finding employment.

That employment found early enough could be the stabilizer that is needed to avoid frustration and temptation.

Each different type of business has their own kinds of issues and finding the right persons to participate in a routine event could make a substantial difference in recidivism.

Particular attention could be done for seasonal employers to help dischargees to build a bit of revenue to help them get traction in the outside world again. When the season is over, the employer sees them go home while the prisoner arrives back home with some dollars that might make the difference in them being able to stay independent.

Repeating the events from year to year could put a real ding in the recidivism problem.

13 - Possible Prisoner Skill Highlighting

Prison tourism could provide an opportunity for prisoners to document their capabilities to present to attendees at the events. The event preparation would also leave the prisoner with documentation that they could hopefully use later in their job search efforts.

Well-formatted documentation could help prisoners to submit their documentation in a progressively enhanced manner, better each year.

The types of things that can be included should highlight all legitimate business skills and experiences that the prisoner would bring to day one on a new job. Every effort should be taken to shape the brand of the person and their optimal effective use which could include;

    Physical Abilities
    Educational Credentials
    Management Experience
    Pastimes
    Family dynamics
    Languages
    Computer Skills
    Drivers' License (If none, training for one.)
    Hobbies
    Networking Abilities

14 - Prison Tourist Family Time Plusses

Tourism could be a well-formatted venue to create a series of opportunities for prisoners and their families and the communities that host the prisons.

Creating a non-threatening format for interaction between deserving prisoners and the world could be a giant step forward for the normalization of relations with the broader society.

A long trip to prison for a short visit with a loved one is probably not really appealing to prisoners families when they are many and the time is small. If the same family had a few days where they could access that same loved one and spend a chunk of time each with the prisoner and the rest of the time with the rest of the family, then the dynamics would be different.

I wrote previously about family visits in:
1. *Prison Possibilities Family Time: A Reason to Thrive!*
2. *Prisoner Family Talks, Days, Stays & Vacations: Connecting Helps Healing*
3. *Prison Segmentation For Family Villages*

15 - Prison Tourism Wrap-Up

Prison Tourism could be a significant opportunity to break free from the stifle of incarceration and start to see oneself in an old but different way. When prisoners can begin to understand and or project themselves in a new light, they can create a series of fresh opportunities for themselves and their families and the communities that they came from and will call home.

Prison Tourism could bring a lot of benefits, but the main factor is a change of thinking.

I will finish with the last two paragraphs from the Angel Raphael Speaks Series Message Set 9 titled "Prison Life of the Future."

" …Please consider as if the vibration of a prison existed on a scale that you could read called the love fear continuum. Consider that a single increment move on that scale that went away from fear and moved towards love was actually beneficial to all who passed through the premises.

As you ever so slightly held that thought, you entertained the possibility for a shift for the imprisoned and guards of the future. Congratulations, for you, have allowed some light to shine on a subject that is almost perpetually locked in pessimism. "

May All Who read This be Blessed,
AND SO IT IS!

16 - Thank You

For
Considering
These
Ideas

17 - Don't Worry Ever

Ever
It Does Not Help Prayer Still Does!

Resource: http://Create-A-Prayer.com

18 - Books Category Resources
at www.Amazon.com

Distant Healing (or Mail List) e-mail mikewann@voicenet.com

Veterans Healing Six Pack plus 2
http://angelraphaelspeaks.com/healing-books/veterans/

PTSD Power Pack
http://angelraphaelspeaks.com/healing-books/ptsd/

Angel Raphael Speaks Series & Other Angel Books
http://angelraphaelspeaks.com/

Reiki
http://angelraphaelspeaks.com/healing-books/reiki/

Children
http://angelraphaelspeaks.com/healing-books/children/

Emergency Medical Kindness
http://angelraphaelspeaks.com/healing-books/emergency-medical-kindness/

Cancer
http://angelraphaelspeaks.com/healing-books/cancer/

Addictions
http://angelraphaelspeaks.com/healing-books/addictions/

Miscellaneous Healing
http://angelraphaelspeaks.com/healing-books/misc-healing/

Prison Books - 50+ Prison Books
http://angelraphaelspeaks.com/prison-books/

19 - Angels Please Prayers

Addict's
Angels of Healing Selected
Help Me to Stay Directed
Come To Me From The Sky
I Am Ready to Succeed Not Try
If I Don't Invite You In
I Might Not Win
I Have Been Lost For Too Long
Help Me To Stay Strong

Alcoholic's
Angels of Healing On High
Help Me to Stay Dry
Come To Me From The Sky
I Am Ready to Succeed Not Try
If I Don't Invite You In
I Might Not Win
I Have Been Lost For Too Long
Help Me To Stay Strong

Prayers Above From

ANGELS ARE ALWAYS
AROUND ADDICTS
AND ALCOHOLICS

HELP IS NEAR NOW!
INVITE IT IN!

REVEREND
MIKE WANNER

http://AngelRaphaelSpeaks.com/AAAAAAA/
The Link Above Has the Core Messages from the book on drop-down pages.

20 - Private Channeling

Angel Raphael Speaks a series of free messages that are channeled through Reverend Mike Wanner for the Highest good and Highest Healing of all concerned.

Many questions arise about Reverend Mike doing private channeling, and he does help with that so E-mail him.

Reverend Mike is available worldwide as a psychic channel, emotional release facilitator, spiritual energy practitioner & teacher, and public speaker.

He looks forward to meeting you soon! Email - mikewann@voicenet.com 215-342-1270

PRIVATE SPIRITUAL READINGS/channelings or Spiritual Healing Sessions: Telephone or in person.

Rev. Mike is available for individual, intuitive one-on-one sessions with you, his Guide Family, and your Guides. He helps by offering clarity on emotional situations about your life, your purpose, your spirituality, and your release of stuffed emotions and cellular memory.

Connect to the love of your Guides today!

For more information, Please visit

http://angelraphaelspeaks.com/channel/

21 - Reverend Mike Wanner

Rev. Mike Wanner started his spiritual and ministerial studies with Reiki in 1993 and had studied seven styles of Reiki in the U.S., Japan, Canada, Denmark, and Australia. He is certified to teach.

He became certified to teach Integrated Energy Therapy in 1999 and co-taught the first IET class of the new Millennium. Mike began dowsing in 2001.

Ordained as an Interfaith Minister of the Circle of Miracles Ministry and a Metaphysical Minister of the International Metaphysical Ministry, Rev. Mike practices and teaches spiritual energy therapies in the Philadelphia Area.

Rev. Mike holds ministerial degrees from the University of Metaphysics and the University of Sedona. He is a Pastoral Care Associate at Jefferson - Frankford Hospital. He taught at the National Academy of Massage Therapy and Health Sciences.

Rev. Mike was a faculty member of the Medical Mission Sister's Center for Human Integration's School of Integrated Body/Mind Therapies in Fox Chase, Philadelphia, PA for twelve years.

For a complete Biography, Please visit

http://ReverendMikeWanner.com/Bio

www.ingramcontent.com/pod-product-compliance
Lightning Source LLC
Chambersburg PA
CBHW030126230526
45469CB00005B/1818